The Mikado
Vocal Score

W. S. Gilbert
and
Sir Arthur Sullivan

New Edition
by Carl Simpson and Ephraim Hammett Jones

With a New Piano Reduction by
Ephraim Hammett Jones

DOVER PUBLICATIONS, INC.
Mineola, New York

Complete performance material for this work is available on rental from:

MMB Music, Inc.
Contemporary Arts Building
3526 Washington Avenue
Saint Louis, Missouri 63132, USA

Phone: 314 531-9635; 800 543-3771 (USA/Canada)
FAX: 314 531-8384
E-mail: mmbmusic@mmbmusic.com
Website: http://www.mmbmusic.com

Copyright

Bibliographical Note

Carl Simpson and Ephraim Hammett Jones' edition of *The Mikado* is a new work, first published by Dover Publications, Inc., in 1999, and in the present vocal score in 2000. Newly engraved plates for both publications were prepared by the editors.

International Standard Book Number: 0-486-41163-X

Manufactured in the United States of America
Dover Publications, Inc., 31 East 2nd Street, Mineola, N.Y. 11501

CONTENTS

ACT ONE
Scene: Courtyard of Ko-Ko's Official Residence

ACT TWO
Scene: Ko-Ko's Garden

PREFACE

The *Mikado*, arguably the greatest masterpiece among the remarkable series of comic operas that came about from the collaboration of playwright William S. Gilbert and composer Sir Arthur S. Sullivan along with the partnership of impresario Richard D'Oyly Carte, had its genesis less than a year after the composer informed Carte of his intention to leave the partnership which had proved so successful in the nine years since the introduction of *Trial By Jury*.

After conducting the premiere of *Princess Ida* on January 5th, 1884, Sullivan collapsed backstage from a combination of exhaustion and a flare-up of his chronic kidney disease. In addition to being depressed by the sudden death of longtime friend Frederic Clay, the composer was dissatisfied with the state of his career following knighthood the year before. The English music establishment of the era simultaneously praised his talent and condemned his 'prostitution' of that talent by working in the field of 'light' or comic opera. Examples of this attitude are to be found in a review of *Iolanthe* which appeared in the *London Globe*: "Mr. Sullivan's music is undoubtedly the work of a masterly musician, content for awhile to partially sacrifice himself rather than hinder the clear enunciation of words . . ." as well as an editorial in the *Musical Review* upon the award of knighthood: "Some things that Mr. Arthur Sullivan may do, Sir Arthur ought not to do. In other words, it will look rather more than odd to see announced in the papers that a new comic opera is in preparation, the book by Mr. W.S. Gilbert and the music by Sir Arthur Sullivan. A musical knight can hardly write shop ballads either; he must not dare to soil his hands with anything less than an anthem or madrigal; oratorio, in which he has so conspicuously shone, and symphony, now must be his line. Here is not only an opportunity, but a positive obligation for his return to the sphere from which he has too long descended." Reviews and editorials such as these exacerbated his bad feelings about not having lived up to his youthful promise—when he was hailed as England's salvation from German domination in the fields of symphonic music and grand opera.

Following a disappointingly short run for *Princess Ida*, Carte, as per their agreement, gave six months' written notification to both the author and composer of their obligation to provide a new work for the Savoy Theatre's fall season. Sullivan, vacationing in Europe at the time, wrote Carte from Brussels: ". . . I ought therefore to tell you at once that it is impossible for me to do another piece of the character of those already written by Gilbert and myself." Gilbert wrote back to inform Sullivan that refusal to write a new work would place him in breach of their agreement. The composer wrote Gilbert to complain that "My tunes are in danger of becoming mere repetitions of my former pieces, my concerted movements are getting to possess a strong family likeness . . ." and to express his frustration with "the words being of such importance that I have been continually keeping down the music." The partnership nearly came to an end shortly after Sullivan's return to London, when Gilbert gave him a 'new' libretto which turned out to be essentially the same as one he had rejected two years earlier in which Gilbert had resorted to using the 'Magic Lozenge Plot'—already made use of in *The Sorcerer* of 1877, which Carte had decided to revive along with *Trial By Jury* in desperation to have something for the fast-approaching fall season.

At about this time, an exhibition opened in London's Knightsbridge district which featured a reproduction of an entire Japanese village. With Japan's recent opening to western trade, a great interest was generated in the West for all things Japanese. By the spring of 1884, the Japanese fashion craze was beginning to reach its zenith in London. After weeks of being at an impasse with Sullivan over the plot for their next opera, Gilbert at last came up with the idea of using a Japanese setting as the gateway for a brilliant satire of English society. The story about the inspiration coming from a Japanese sword falling from the wall of Gilbert's study may be partly true: Gilbert mentioned the sword in an 1895 interview with a New York paper—though nothing is said about the sword falling off the wall. Gilbert's likely observation of the great interest generated by the Knightsbridge exhibit no doubt played a role as well. When Gilbert informed Sullivan of his new Japanese idea, the composer was greatly relieved and accepted the new plot sight unseen.

The new libretto was not given to Sullivan until some six months later (on November 20, 1884). At that time Gilbert presented the composer with the first act for consideration. By December 8th, Sullivan was at work on the music. The first number composed was Pish-Tush's solo in Act One, "Our Great Mikado, Virtuous Man." Sullivan worked at a furious pace on the opera through February and March of 1885. On March 3rd, his diary entry reported: "Worked all night at finale, 1st act. finished 5 a.m. 63 pages of score at one sitting!" Sullivan even incorporated a genuine Japanese soldiers' song in the work ("Mi-ya Sa-ma" Entrance of the Mikado, Act Two).

Though rehearsals were under way by early February, both he and Gilbert continued to revise and polish the work until a week before opening night. The overture was created in the space of 30 hours by Sullivan's associate Hamilton Clarke per the composer's instructions shortly before the premiere. The premiere, on March 14, 1885, was a tremendous success with audience and critics alike. The initial run at the Savoy Theatre was a record 672 performances. Although the two men's relationship was never more than one of cordial professionalism, the resolution of the conflict from the previous year gave their partnership new life. The operas *Ruddigore* (1887), *The Yeoman of the Guard* (1888), and *The Gondoliers* (1889) came about as a result of this restoration. The partnership finally collapsed in 1891 after Gilbert filed a lawsuit against Carte and Sullivan. After its resolution, Carte managed to persuade the composer to work with Gilbert again for the unsuccessful works *Utopia Limited* (1893) and *The Grand Duke* (1896). Sullivan died at his London apartment in November of 1900.

With its witty text, engaging music and brilliant orchestration, *The Mikado* has deservedly enjoyed enormous popularity in the 114 years since its creation. In addition to setting a record for consecutive performances not broken until 1922, it was the first of the operas to be recorded on disk (in 1907). It is nearly unique among the Gilbert and Sullivan operas in that it has achieved popularity even in countries where English is not widely spoken. The opera has been translated and performed in German, Italian, Russian, and Hungarian, to name a few. The vocal score was first published by Chappell in 1885. An authorized American vocal score ("arrangement for pianoforte by George Lowell Tracy"—a student of Sullivan's) was issued the same year by William A. Pond & Co. of New York. The full score first appeared in 1898, issued by the Leipzig office of Bosworth & Co.

For the present edition, the primary sources consulted include: The autograph full score, including Hamilton Clarke's Overture, as published in facsimile by Gregg in 1968; the Bosworth full score mentioned above—in an undated reprint by E.F. Kalmus; the Chappell and Pond vocal scores (Chappell in a ca. 1911 reprint, Pond in a very early—possibly first—printing); and two 1885 American libretti: the first issued by Pond (listing the cast of the August 19, 1885 "official" American premiere at the Fifth Street Theatre in New York); the second, issued by H. Grau, New York, claiming to be "Reprinted from the English libretto published and sold by CHAPPELL & CO. in London." (a pirate edition?). The presence of an autographer's castoff marks (in German) exactly matching the pagination of the Bosworth full score clearly point to Sullivan's manuscript as the primary source material used to produce the 1898 publication. In light of the speed at which it was written, the autograph score, not surprisingly, is loaded with abbreviations. Page after page of the score features a single vocal line, along with some shorthand indications in the adjacent empty staves to copy passages from previous sections of the music. Presumably, because of the cost involved, the Bosworth score was actually photo-offset from an autographer's pen-and-ink fair copy. Interestingly, the text that appears in this full score closely matches that in the autograph; a number of the revisions made by Gilbert just prior to the first performance—certainly before the issue of the vocal score—were not incorporated into the 1898 score. A few other items that were penciled in the autograph, such as the bassoon solo in mm. 42 and 79 of "Three Little Maids from School," are curiously absent from both the vocal scores and the Bosworth full score. Apart from the errors mentioned and a fair number of wrong notes and articulation/phrasing inaccuracies, the above scores represented, for their time, fairly accurate readings of the composer's manuscript. Perhaps their greatest shortcomings lie in their tight spacing of both music and libretto that is not always immediately readable and a layout and design that is often inconvenient to the performer.

While the present edition is intended as one for practical performance instead of a critical edition in the strict sense of the term, great effort has been taken to present a score that is accurate to the composer's intentions. Numerous wrong notes, articulation/phrasing and textual inconsistencies appearing in the early scores have been corrected without comment from the manuscript or from analogous passages elsewhere in the manuscript or first edition vocal score. The piano reduction is entirely new and incorporates additional musical elements not found in previous versions. Items inserted by the editors to facilitate performance, or that have come down to the present day from the long-standing performance tradition, have either been set in cue-sized notes, placed in brackets, or marked with an asterisk and footnoted. Special care has been taken to make the present score as practical and readable as possible from a performer's view in terms of its overall layout and design. The editors wish to express their gratitude to pianist Steven Lichtenstein for reading through the new reduction and his helpful suggestions. It is hoped that this new score to be of benefit to performers, students, music lovers and Gilbert & Sullivan fans everywhere in their enjoyment and appreciation of this most delightful and accessible work.

Carl Simpson
Ephraim Hammett Jones
Spring, 2000

DRAMATIS PERSONÆ

THE MIKADO OF JAPAN .... BASS

NANKI-POO (His son, disguised as a wandering minstrel; in love with Yum-Yum) .... TENOR

KO-KO (Lord High Executioner of Titipu) .... BARITONE

POOH-BAH (Lord High Everything Else) .... BARITONE

PISH-TUSH (A Noble Lord) .... BASS

YUM-YUM (Ward of Ko-Ko) .... SOPRANO

PITTI-SING (Ward of Ko-Ko, sister of Yum-Yum) .... MEZZO-SOPRANO

PEEP-BO (Ward of Ko-Ko, sister of Yum-Yum and Pitti-Sing) .... MEZZO-SOPRANO

KATISHA (an elderly Lady, in love with Nanki-Poo) .... CONTRALTO

CHORUS OF NOBLES, SCHOOLGIRLS, GUARDS AND SERVANTS

ORIGINAL CAST

THE MIKADO OF JAPAN .... Mr. R. Temple

NANKI-POO .... Mr. Durward Lely

KO-KO .... Mr. George Grossmith

POOH-BAH .... Mr. Rutland Barrington

PISH-TUSH .... Mr. Frederick Bovill

YUM-YUM .... Miss Leonora Braham

PITTI-SING .... Miss Jessie Bond

PEEP-BO .... Miss Sybil Grey

KATISHA .... Miss Rossina Brandram

CHORUS OF THE D'OYLY CARTE OPERA COMPANY
SIR ARTHUR SULLIVAN, CONDUCTOR
RICHARD D'OYLY CARTE, MANAGER; W.S. GILBERT, DIRECTOR

SYNOPSIS

The opera opens with the noblemen of Titipu gathered at the courtyard of the Lord High Executioner's palace; they strike ceremonial attitudes and noble poses similar to those that are found "on many a vase and jar, on many a screen and fan." Into this highly formal scene rushes Nanki-Poo, a poor, threadbare, wandering minstrel carrying a 'native guitar' on his back and a bundle of ballads in his hand; he asks excitedly about the whereabouts of Yum-Yum, a lovely young woman who is the ward of Ko-Ko (the Lord High Executioner). When asked to identify himself, Nanki-Poo boasts of his ability to supply a song for any possible occasion: sentimental songs to charm the ladies, patriotic war songs for the troops, sea-chanties for the sailors, etc. He goes on to explain that while playing second trombone in the town band some months ago, he had fallen madly in love with Yum-Yum, whose guardian was Ko-Ko, a cheap tailor. After finding out that Ko-Ko had decided to marry Yum-Yum himself, he left Titipu in despair. When the news reached him that Ko-Ko had been sentenced to decapitation for the crime of flirting, Nanki-Poo hurried back to Titipu in order to propose to Yum-Yum. He considered Ko-Ko's objections to be irrelevant, since the tailor was in jail awaiting execution.

Upon hearing this, the noble Pish-Tush relates to Nanki-Poo the tale of Ko-Ko's elevation from cheap tailor to Lord High Executioner of Titipu. It seems that when the great Mikado issued his decree requiring decapitation for the crime of flirting, the nobles of Titipu became alarmed at how easy it would be for any of them to end up headless (flirtation being such a natural act). Accordingly, they devised the perfect scheme to circumvent the new decree: Ko-Ko would be appointed Lord High Executioner. After all, he was the first to be sentenced under the new law and would therefore have to cut off his own head before carrying out the sentence upon anyone else! With his appointment, however, the noblemen could no longer serve as public officials since Ko-Ko was a mere tailor. Fortunately for Titipu, Pooh-Bah, the only public official left, was of pre-Adamite descent and was able to humble himself in order to take over all of the now vacant positions—along with all of the salaries. Thus Pooh-Bah became Lord High Everything Else. Only after agreeing to accept Nanki-Poo's pitifully small bribe do Pooh-Bah and Pish-Tush inform him that Yum-Yum is scheduled to marry the Lord High Executioner that very afternoon.

Nanki-Poo leaves to contemplate this situation, and the Lord High Executioner arrives with great fanfare to plan his upcoming week-long wedding celebrations. To further impress the gathered nobles of the importance—and permanence—of his new title he lets them know that "as someday it may happen that a victim must be found, I've got a little list!" Ko-Ko dismisses the nobles and confers with Pooh-Bah, who gives the Executioner conflicting advice from several of the official positions he now holds. Naturally, the confusion is settled only after Ko-Ko's payment of an enormous bribe. They leave quickly so as not to be spotted by Yum-Yum and her two sisters, Pitti-Sing and Peep-Bo, who, along with their classmates, are returning from the ladies finishing school. Nevertheless, Ko-Ko is unable to resist Yum-Yum's great beauty and rushes over to greet her with a kiss. Yum-Yum winces and runs away with her sisters to greet Nanki-Poo when they notice him standing at the courtyard's edge. The three sisters try to properly introduce Nanki-Poo to the Lord High Executioner; but Ko-Ko quickly has the young man chased away in order to introduce them to Pooh-Bah. Pooh-Bah, not accustomed to speaking with anyone below the rank of Stockbroker, doesn't have the slightest interest in speaking to these schoolgirls, who make fun of him anyway. He greets them, at great expense to his pride, only after some chiding from Ko-Ko. The girls apologize to Pooh-Bah and even invite him to "dance and sing" along with them. Pooh-Bah dances off with Peep-Bo and Pitti-Sing, leaving Yum-Yum alone in the courtyard. Nanki-Poo returns to express his great love for her and reveals that he is not an itinerant musician but is in fact the Mikado's son. He has run away from his father's court to escape the elderly Katisha, who, having mistaken his simple kindness as a wedding proposal, is now claiming the title of "daughter-in-law elect." Likewise, Yum-Yum confesses her utter misery in having to marry Ko-Ko. The two lovers move ever closer—finally stealing an illegal kiss before leaving in opposite directions.

Arriving just in time to see Yum-Yum walking away in the distance, Ko-Ko sighs wistfully —only to be interrupted by Pooh-Bah and Pish-Tush, who holds a letter addressed to Ko-Ko from the Mikado. The ruler is most concerned that no executions have taken place in Titipu for over a year. He has furthermore given orders requiring an execution to be performed in a month's time. Should Ko-Ko fail in his duty to carry out this order, the Mikado promises to abolish the post of Lord High Executioner. Accordingly, the status of Titipu will then be reduced from town to that of village. Pooh-Bah is quick to point out that Ko-Ko is the most logical candidate for execution since he was already sentenced under the Mikado's flirtation laws. He further urges that Ko-Ko, as Lord High Executioner, make the sacrifice for the good of the town. Ko-Ko protests that he is simply not capable of cutting off his own head and suggests that Pooh-Bah be appointed Lord High Substitute in his place. Pooh-Bah declines this appointment on the grounds that he must "set bounds to my insatiable ambition." All the while Pish-Tush is encouraging either of them to volunteer since "criminals who are cut in two can hardly feel the fatal steel." The three are reduced to admitting their dread of "awaiting the sensation of a short, sharp, shock" before Pooh-Bah and Pish-Tush leave Ko-Ko to mourn his probable fate. Just then, to Ko-Ko's good fortune, Nanki-Poo walks past him carrying a rope while threatening suicide over his being unable to marry Yum-Yum. Ko-Ko promptly takes full advantage of this situation by persuading Nanki-Poo to accept execution in return for a one-month marriage to Yum-Yum. It appears the perfect solution to everyone's problems: Nanki-Poo and Yum-Yum can be married; Ko-Ko can marry Yum-Yum later, after she becomes a widow; Titipu will at last be able to satisfy the Mikado's demand for an execution. The ensuing celebration is disrupted by the unexpected appearance of Katisha, who has been diligently searching for the object of her passion, Nanki-Poo. Though she keeps Nanki-Poo from running off with Yum-Yum to be married and nearly turns the entire town against him with her story, Katisha is ultimately drowned-out by the crowd as she attempts to betray Nanki-Poo's true identity. Thus spurned, she vows revenge before her melodramatic departure from Titipu.

The second act opens in Ko-Ko's garden, where Yum-Yum is being decorated and dressed for her wedding to Nanki-Poo. Though everything is joyful on the surface, the underlying mood of all present becomes more and more somber—even after Nanki-Poo and Pish-Tush arrive and try to raise their spirits. They are simply unable to subdue their thoughts of the happy bride becoming a widow after one short month. With Ko-Ko's arrival there is even worse news: he has discovered that the law, still in effect, requires the wife of an executed criminal to be buried alive. Neither Yum-Yum or Ko-Ko can bear the thought of such a thing, and the wedding is called off. Nanki-Poo then returns to his original plan of committing suicide. Ko-Ko argues to no avail that Nanki-Poo must honor the agreement to be executed in any case, becoming even more desperate when he is notified that the Mikado himself is on the way to Titipu. Nanki-Poo calls his bluff by challenging Ko-Ko to decapitate him then and there, an event which would satisfy Pooh-Bah's interest as well. Ko-Ko makes excuse after excuse for not lifting the sword before admitting that he is incapable of killing anything. With the Mikado fast approaching, Ko-Ko and Pooh-Bah hurriedly concoct a scheme whereby Pooh-Bah (for a huge bribe, of course) will issue a phony affidavit testifying to Nanki-Poo's execution. Pooh-Bah, also serving as the Archbishop of Titipu, will then marry Nanki-Poo and Yum-Yum, who must promise to leave town at once and never return.

As the plan is being carried out, the imperial procession arrives with the troops chanting the Japanese war-song "Mi-ya Sa-ma." The Mikado enters Titipu along with the "daughter-in-law elect," Katisha, whose boastful proclamations upstage the emperor's own at every turn. The Mikado subsequently explains to the residents of Titipu his overall philosophy of law and justice, the most important principle of which is "to make the punishment fit the crime." Upon hearing this, Ko-Ko hands over to the appreciative Mikado the affidavit describing the execution of a certain wandering minstrel, duly signed by all of the acting public officials (Pooh-Bah). At the Mikado's request, Pooh-Bah, Ko-Ko and Pitti-Sing then proceed to describe the execution of the minstrel in gruesome detail. Much to their horror, the emperor then explains that the true purpose of his visit is to find his missing son, who plays second trombone and uses the name Nanki-Poo. When Katisha notices Nanki-Poo's name on the affidavit of execution, Ko-Ko and his accomplices all try to explain their way out of this apparent act of regicide. The Mikado, in keeping with his judicial philosophy, cheerfully sentences the three to a death by means of "something lingering, with boiling oil in it." With things now in a truly disastrous state, Ko-Ko runs to find the newly married couple, who have not yet left town, in order to beg Nanki-Poo to show himself to his father and spare the lives of the conspirators. Nanki-Poo agrees to do so only on the condition that Ko-Ko marry the vindictive Katisha, who is now quite brokenhearted at being "Alone and yet alive." The wary Ko-Ko approaches her with much caution to confess that he has long held a secret passion for her and will surely die of a broken heart if she rejects him now. With this, Katisha at last melts and agrees to marry Ko-Ko after discovering that they share some bizarre tastes in common for things such as "the tiger a-lashing of his tail and the flight of thunderbolts." With Katisha safely married to Ko-Ko, Nanki-Poo reveals himself to his father, who wisely forgives the trickery of Ko-Ko and company. All then join in the celebration for the happy couple to end the opera.

INSTRUMENTATION

2 FLUTES
(2ND DOUBLES PICCOLO)
OBOE
2 CLARINETS IN B-FLAT
BASSOON

2 HORNS IN F
2 CORNETS IN B-FLAT
2 TROMBONES

TIMPANI
PERCUSSION:
TRIANGLE, CYMBALS,
SNARE DRUM, BASS DRUM
(1 PLAYER)

VIOLIN I
VIOLIN II
VIOLA
VIOLONCELLO
CONTRABASS

Duration: ca. 90 minutes

Premiere: March 14, 1885
Savoy Theatre, London, England
D'Oyly Carte Opera Company,
Orchestra and Chorus
Sir Arthur Sullivan, conductor

Complete performance material for this work is available on rental from:

MMB Music, Inc.
Contemporary Arts Building
3526 Washington Avenue
Saint Louis, Missouri 63103, USA
Phone: 314 531-9635; 800 543-3771 (US/Canada)
FAX: 314 531-8384
E-mail: mmbmusic@mmbmusic.com
Website: http://www.mmbmusic.com

THE MIKADO

or
The Town of Titipu

Overture

William S. Gilbert

Sir Arthur Sullivan

Allegro Moderato

3

Act One

Scene: Courtyard of Ko-Ko's Palace in Titipu. Japanese nobles discovered standing and sitting in attitudes suggested by native drawings.

Nº 1. Chorus: "If You Want to Know Who We Are"
Noblemen of Titipu

18

vase and jar, On screen and fan.

vase and jar, On screen and fan.

Enter Nanki-Poo in great excitment. He carries a native guitar on his back and a bundle of ballads in his hand.

Nº 2. Song and Chorus "A Wandering Minstrel I"

Nanki-Poo and Noblemen

N-Poo: fied! Our war-ri-ors, in ser-ried ranks as - sem - bled, Ne - ver

N-Poo: quail– or they con-ceal it if they do— And I should-n't be sur-prised if na - tions

N-Poo: trem - bled Be-fore the might-y troops, the troops of Ti - ti - pu!

T.
Chor.: We should-n't be sur-prised if

B.: We should-n't be sur-prised if

ho, heave ho, Yeo ho, heave ho, heave ho, heave ho, yeo - ho!

ho, heave ho, Yeo ho, heave ho, heave ho, heave ho, yeo - ho!

Allegretto (come Iº)
114 **Tempo Iº**

A

wan - d'ring min - strel I— A thing of shreds and patch - es, Of bal - lads, songs, and

(Enter Pish-Tush)

P-Tush: And what may be your business with Yum-Yum?

N-Poo: I'll tell you. A year ago I was a member of the Titipu town band. It was my duty to take the cap round for contributions. While discharging this delicate office, I saw Yum-Yum. We loved each other at once, but she was betrothed to her guardian, Ko-Ko, a cheap tailor, and I saw that my suit was hopeless. Overwhelmed with despair, I quitted the town. Judge of my delight when I heard, a month ago, that Ko-Ko had been condemned to death for flirting! I hurried back at once, in the hope of finding Yum-Yum at liberty to listen to my protestations.

P-Tush: It is true that Ko-Ko was condemned to death for flirting, but he was reprieved at the last moment, and raised to the exalted rank of Lord High Executioner under the following remarkable circumstances:

Nº 3. Song and Chorus "Our Great Mikado, Virtuous Man"

Pish-Tush and Noblemen

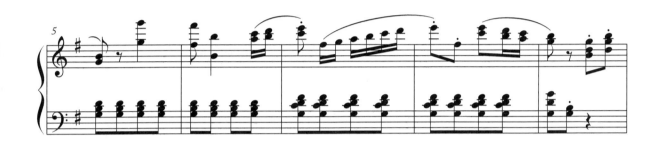

Our great Mi - ka - do, vir - tuous man, When he to rule our

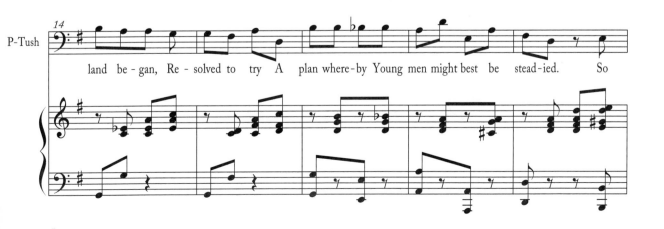

land be - gan, Re - solved to try A plan where - by Young men might best be stead - ied. So

This stern de-cree, you'll un-der-stand, Caused great dis-may through-

out the land: For young and old And shy and bold Were e-qual-ly af-fect-ed. The

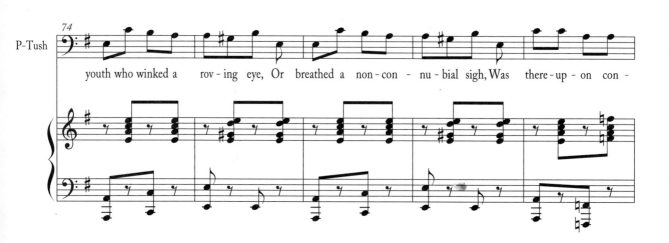

youth who winked a rov-ing eye, Or breathed a non-con-nu-bial sigh, Was there-up-on con-

(Exeunt Chorus. Enter Pooh-Bah.)

N-Poo: Ko-Ko, the cheap tailor, Lord High Executioner of Titipu! Why, that's the highest rank a citizen can attain!

P-Bah: It is. Our logical Mikado, seeing no moral difference between the dignified judge who condemns a criminal to die, and the industrious mechanic who carries out the sentence, has rolled the two offices into one, and every judge is now his own executioner.

N-Poo: But how good of you (for I see that you are a nobleman of the highest rank) to condescend to tell all this to me, a mere strolling minstrel!

P-Bah: Don't mention it. I am, in point of fact, a particularly haughty and exclusive person, of pre-Adamite ancestral descent. You will understand this when I tell you that I can trace my ancestry back to a protoplasmal primordial atomic globule. Consequently, my family pride is something inconceivable. I can't help it. I was born sneering. But I struggle hard to overcome this defect. I mortify my pride continually. When all the great Officers of State resigned in a body because they were too proud to serve under an ex-tailor, did I not unhesitatingly accept all their posts at once?

P-Tush: And the salaries attached to them? You did.

P-Bah: It is consequently my degrading duty to serve this upstart as First Lord of the Treasury, Lord Chief Justice, Commander-in-Chief, Lord High Admiral, Master of the Buckhounds, Groom of the Back Stairs, Archbishop of Titipu, and Lord Mayor, both acting and elect, all rolled into one. And at a salary! A Pooh-Bah paid for his services! I a salaried minion! But I do it! It revolts me, but I do it.

N-Poo: And it does you credit.

P-Bah: But I don't stop at that. I go and dine with middle-class people on reasonable terms. I dance at cheap suburban parties for a moderate fee. I accept refreshment at any hands, however lowly. I also retail State secrets at a very low figure. For instance, any further information about Yum-Yum would come under the head of a State secret.
(Nanki-Poo takes the hint, and gives him money.)
(Aside), Another insult, and I think a light one!

Nº 4. Song: "Young Man, Despair"

Pooh-Bah, Nanki-Poo, Pish-Tush

44

(Exit Pish-Tush)

(*Exeunt Pooh-Bah and Nanki-Poo. Enter Chorus of Nobles.*)

Nº 5. Chorus and Song: "Behold the Lord High Executioner"

Ko-Ko and Noblemen

Ko-Ko: Gentlemen, I'm much touched by this reception. I can only trust that by strict attention to duty I shall ensure a continuance of those favours which it will ever be my study to deserve. If I should ever be called upon to act professionally, I am happy to think that there will be no difficulty in finding plenty of people whose loss will be a distinct gain to society at large.

Nº 5a. Song: "I've Got a Little List"

Ko-Ko and Noblemen

Ko-Ko: And that

Chor. T.: got her on the list; And I don't think she'll be missed— I'm *sure* she'll not be missed!

B.: got her on the list; And I don't think she'll be missed— I'm *sure* she'll not be missed!

56

Ko-Ko: *Ni - si Pri - us* nui-sance, who just now is ra-ther rife, The Ju - di-cial hu-mor-ist— I've

Ko-Ko: got *him* on the list! All fun - ny fel-lows, com-ic men, and clowns of pri-vate life— They'd

62

(Exeunt Chorus. Enter Pooh-Bah.)

Ko-Ko: Pooh-Bah, it seems that the festivities in connection with my approaching marriage must last a week. I should like to do it handsomely, and I want to consult you as to the amount I ought to spend upon them.

P-Bah: Certainly. In which of my capacities? As First Lord of the Treasury, Lord Chamberlain, Attorney-General, Chancellor of the Exchequer, Privy Purse, or Private Secretary?

Ko-Ko: Suppose we say as Private Secretary.

P-Bah: Speaking as your Private Secretary, I should say that as the city will have to pay for it, don't stint yourself, do it well.

Ko-Ko: Exactly — as the city will have to pay for it. That is your advice.

P-Bah: As Private Secretary. Of course you will understand that, as Chancellor of the Exchequer, I am bound to see that due economy is observed.

Ko-Ko: Oh! But you said just now "Don't stint yourself, do it well".

P-Bah: As Private Secretary.

Ko-Ko: And now you say that due economy must be observed.

P-Bah: As Chancellor of the Exchequer.

Ko-Ko: I see. Come over here, where the Chancellor can't hear us. *(They cross the stage.)* Now, as my Solicitor, how do you advise me to deal with this difficulty?

P-Bah: Oh, as your Solicitor, I should have no hesitation in saying "Chance it—"

Ko-Ko: Thank you. *(Shaking his hand)* I will.

P-Bah: If it were not that, as Lord Chief Justice, I am bound to see that the law isn't violated.

Ko-Ko: I see. Come over here, where the Chief Justice can't hear us. *(They cross the stage.)* Now, then, as First Lord of the Treasury?

P-Bah: Of course, as First Lord of the Treasury, I could propose a special vote that would cover all expenses, if it were not that, as Leader of the Opposition, it would be my duty to resist it, tooth and nail. Or, as Paymaster-General, I could so cook the accounts that, as Lord High Auditor, I should never discover the fraud. But then, as Archbishop of Titipu, it would be my duty to denounce my dishonesty and give myself into my own custody as First Commissioner of Police.

Ko-Ko: That's extremely awkward.

P-Bah: I don't say that all these distinguished people couldn't be squared; but it is right to tell you that they wouldn't be sufficiently degraded in their own estimation unless they are insulted with a very considerable bribe.

Ko-Ko: The matter shall have my careful consideration. But my bride and her sisters approach, and any little compliment on your part, such as an abject grovel in a characteristic Japanese attitude would be esteemed a favour.

(Exeunt together. Enter procession of Yum-Yum's school fellows, heralding Yum-Yum, Peep-Bo, and Pitti-Sing.)

Nº 6. Chorus: "Comes a Train of Little Ladies"
Schoolgirls of Titipu

Nº 7. Trio: "Three Little Maids from School"
Yum-Yum, Peep-Bo, Pitti-Sing and Schoolgirls

18

Y-Yum: glee, ____ Three lit-tle maids from school! Ev-'ry-thing is a source of ____ fun— *(Chuckle)*

P-Bo: glee, ____ Three lit-tle maids from school!

P-Sing: glee, ____ Three lit-tle maids from school!

Peep-Bo:

P-Bo: No-bod-y's safe, for we care for ____ none! *(Chuckle)*

Pitti-Sing:

P-Sing: Life is a joke that's ____ just be - gun! *(Chuckle)*

78

(Enter Ko-Ko and Pooh Bah.)

Ko-Ko: At last, my bride that is to be! *(About to embrace her)*

Y-Yum: You're not going to kiss me before all these people!

Ko-Ko: Well, that was the idea.

Y-Yum: *(Aside to Peep-Bo)* It seems odd, doesn't it?

P-Bo: It's rather peculiar.

P-Sing: Oh, I expect it's all right. Must have a beginning, you know.

Y-Yum: Well, of course I know nothing about these things; but I've no objection if it's usual.

Ko-Ko: Oh, it's quite usual, I think. Eh, Lord Chamberlain? *(Appealing to Poo-Bah)*

P-Bah: I have known it done. *(Ko-Ko embraces her.)*

Y-Yum: Thank goodness that's over! *(Sees Nanki-Poo and rushes to him)* Why, that's never you!

(The three girls rush to him and shake his hands, all speaking at once.)

Y-Yum: Oh, I'm so glad! I haven't seen you for ever so long, and I'm right at the top of the school, and I've got three prizes, and I've come home for good, and I'm not going back any more!

P-Bo: And have you got an engagement? Yum-Yum's got one, but she doesn't like it, and she'd ever so much rather it was you. I've come home for good, and I'm not going back any more!

P-Sing: Now tell us all the news, because you go about everywhere, and we've been at school, but, thank goodness, that's all over now, and we've come home for good, and we're not going back any more!

(These three speeches are spoken together in one breath.)

Ko-Ko: I beg your pardon. Will you present me?

Y-Yum: Oh, this is the musician who used —

P-Bo: Oh, this is the gentleman who used —

P-Sing: Oh, it is only Nanki-Poo who used —

Ko-Ko: One at a time, if you please.

Y-Yum: Oh, if you please, he's the gentleman who used to play so beautifully on the — on the —

P-Sing: On the Marine Parade.

Y-Yum: Yes, I think that was the name of the instrument.

N-Poo: Sir, I have the misfortune to love your ward, Yum-Yum — oh, I know I deserve your anger!

Ko-Ko: Anger! not a bit, my boy. Why, I love her myself. Charming little girl, isn't she? Pretty eyes, nice hair. Taking little thing, altogether. Very glad to hear my opinion backed by a competent authority. Thank you very much. Good-bye. *(To Pish-Tush)* Take him away. *(Pish-Tush removes him.)*

P-Sing: *(Who has been examining Pooh-Bah)* I beg your pardon, but what is this? Customer come to try on?

Ko-Ko: That is a Tremendous Swell.

P-Sing: Oh, it's alive. *(She starts back in alarm.)*

P-Bah: Go away, little girls. Can't talk to little girls like you. Go away, there's dears.

Ko-Ko: Allow me to present you, Pooh-Bah. These are my three wards. The one in the middle is my bride-elect.

P-Bah: What do you want me to do to them? Mind, I *will not* kiss them.

Ko-Ko: No, no, you shan't kiss them: a little bow — a mere nothing — you needn't mean it, you know.

P-Bah: It goes against the grain. They are not young ladies, they are young persons.

Ko-Ko: Come, come, make an effort, there's a good nobleman.

P-Bah: *(Aside to Ko-Ko)* Well, I shan't mean it. *(With a great effort)* How de do, little girls, how de do? *(Aside)* Oh, my protoplasmal ancestor!

Ko-Ko: That's very good. *(Girls indulge in suppressed laughter.)*

P-Bah: I see nothing to laugh at. It is very painful to me to have to say "How de do, little girls, how de do?" to young persons. I'm not in the habit of saying "How de do, little girls, how de do?" to anybody under the rank of a Stockbroker.

Ko-Ko: *(Aside to girls)* Don't laugh at him, he can't help it — he's under treatment for it. *(Aside to Pooh-Bah)* Never mind them, they don't understand the delicacy of your position.

P-Bah: We know how delicate it is, don't we?

Ko-Ko: I should think we did! How a nobleman of your importance can do it at all is a thing I never can, never shall understand.

(Ko-Ko retires up and goes off.)

*Nº 8. Quintett: "So Please You, Sir, We Much Regret"
Yum-Yum, Peep-Bo, Pitti-Sing, Pooh-Bah, Pish-Tush and Schoolgirls

* This number is often performed as a quartet by omitting Pish-Tush's line.

* Early vocal scores assign this line to Pish-Tush. Autograph indication reads: "Pish-Tush still tacet".

(Exeunt all but Yum-Yum. Enter Nanki-Poo.)

N-Poo: Yum-Yum, at last we are alone! I have sought you night and day for three weeks, in the belief that your guardian was beheaded, and I find that you are about to be married to him this afternoon!

Y-Yum: Alas, yes!

N-Poo: But you do not love him?

Y-Yum: Alas, no!

N-Poo: Modified rapture! But why do you not refuse him?

Y-Yum: What good would that do? He's my guardian, and he wouldn't let me marry you.

N-Poo: But I would wait until you were of age!

Y-Yum: You forget that in Japan girls do not arrive at years of discretion until they are fifty.

N-Poo: True; from seventeen to forty-nine are considered years of indiscretion.

Y-Yum: Besides — a wandering minstrel, who plays a wind instrument outside tea-houses, is hardly a fitting husband for the ward of a Lord High Executioner.

N-Poo: But— *(Aside)* Shall I tell her? Yes! She will not betray me! *(Aloud)* What if it should prove that, after all, I am no musician!

Y-Yum: There! I was certain of it, directly I heard you play!

N-Poo: What if it should prove that I am no other than the son of his Majesty the Mikado?

Y-Yum: The son of the Mikado! But why is your highness disguised? And what has your Highness done? And will your Highness promise never to do it again?

N-Poo: Some years ago I had the misfortune to captivate Katisha, an elderly lady of my father's Court. She misconstrued my customary affability into expressions of affection, and claimed me in marriage, under my father's law. My father, the Lucius Junius Brutus of his race, ordered me to marry her within a week, or perish ignominiously on the scaffold. That night I fled his Court, and, assuming the disguise of a Second Trombone, I joined the band in which you found me when I had the happiness of seeing you! *(Approaching her)*

Y-Yum: *(Retreating)* If you please, I think your Highness had better not come too near. The laws against flirting are excessively severe.

N-Poo: But we are quite alone, and nobody can see us.

Y-Yum: Still, that doesn't make it right. To flirt is capital.

N-Poo: It *is* capital!

Y-Yum: And we must obey the law.

N-Poo: Deuce take the law!

Y-Yum: I wish it would, but it won't!

N-Poo: If it were not for that, how happy we might be!

Y-Yum: Happy indeed!

N-Poo: If it were not for the law, we should now be sitting side by side, like that. *(Sits by her)*

Y-Yum: Instead of being obliged to sit half a mile off, like that. *(Crosses and sits at other side of stage)*

N-Poo: We should be gazing into each other's eyes, like that.
        (Approaching and gazing at her sentimentally)

Y-Yum: Breathing sighs of unutterable love — like that. *(Sighing and gazing lovingly at him)*

N-Poo: With our arms round each other's waists, like that. *(Embracing her)*

Y-Yum: Yes, if it wasn't for the law.

N-Poo: If it wasn't for the law.

Y-Yum: As it is, of course we couldn't do anything of the kind.

N-Poo; Not for worlds!

Y-Yum: Being engaged to Ko-Ko, you know!

N-Poo: Being engaged to Ko-Ko!

Nº 9. Duet: "Were I Not to Ko-Ko Plighted"

Yum-Yum, Nanki-Poo

* To perform the traditional abridged version cut from m. 2 to m. 58 on p. 92.

* For the abridged version of this duet the lyrics in italics should be sung.

merge all rank and sta-tion, World-ly sneers are nought to us. And, to mark— my ad-mi-

Y-Yum
He would kiss me fond-ly thus! (Kiss)

N-Poo
ra-tion, I would kiss you fond-ly thus— I would kiss you fond-ly thus! (Kissing her)

Allegro

Y-Yum
But as I'm en-gaged to Ko-Ko, To em-brace you thus, con fuo-co, Would dis-tinct-ly be no gio-co

N-Poo
But as you're en-gaged to Ko-Ko, To em-brace you thus, con fuo-co, Would dis-tinct-ly be no gio-co,

Allegro

* For the abridged version of this duet Yum-Yum sings mm. 76–95 instead of Nanki-Poo.

94

* For the abridged version the lyrics in italics should be sung in mm. 96–99.

(Exeunt in opposite directions. Enter Ko-Ko.)

Ko-Ko: *(Looking after Yum-Yum)* There she goes! To think how entirely my future happiness is wrapped up in that little parcel! Really, it hardly seems worth while! Oh, matrimony!— *(Enter Pooh-Bah and Pish-Tush.)* Now then, what is it? Can't you see I'm soliloquizing? You have interrupted an apostrophe, sir!

P-Tush: I am the bearer of a letter from his Majesty, the Mikado.

Ko-Ko: *(Taking it from him reverentially)* A letter from the Mikado! What in the world can he have to say to me? *(Reads letter)* Ah, here it is at last! I thought it would come sooner or later! The Mikado is struck by the fact that no executions have taken place in Titipu for a year, and decrees that unless somebody is beheaded within one month, the post of Lord High Executioner shall be abolished, and the city reduced to the rank of a village!

P-Tush: But that will involve us all in irretrievable ruin!

Ko-Ko: Yes. There is no help for it, I shall have to execute somebody at once. The only question is, who shall it be?

P-Bah: Well, it seems unkind to say so, but as you're already under sentence of death for flirting, everything seems to point to *you*.

Ko-Ko: To me? What are you talking about? I can't execute myself.

P-Bah: Why not?

Ko-Ko: Why not? Because, in the first place, self-decapitation is an extremely difficult, not to say dangerous, thing to attempt; and, in the second, it's suicide, and suicide is a capital offense.

P-Bah: That is so, no doubt.

P-Tush: We might reserve that point.

P-Bah: True, it could be argued six months hence, before the full Court.

Ko-Ko: Besides, I don't see how a man *can* cut off his own head.

P-Bah A man might try.

P-Tush: Even if you only succeeded in cutting it half off, that would be something.

P-Bah: It would be taken as an earnest of your desire to comply with the Imperial will.

Ko-Ko: No. Pardon me, but there I am adamant. As official Headsman, my reputation is at stake, and I can't consent to embark on a professional operation unless I see my way to a successful result.

P-Bah: This professional conscientiousness is highly creditable to *you*, but it places us in a very awkward position.

Ko-Ko: My good sir, the awkwardness of your position is grace itself compared with that of a man engaged in the act of cutting off his own head.

P-Tush: I am afraid that, unless you can obtain a substitute—

Ko-Ko: A substitute? Oh, certainly — nothing easier. *(To Pooh-Bah)* Pooh-Bah, I appoint you Lord High Substitute.

P-Bah: I should be delighted. Such an appointment would realize my fondest dreams. But no, at any sacrifice, I must set bounds to my insatiable ambition!

Nº 10. Trio: "I Am So Proud"
Pooh-Bah, Ko-Ko and Pish-Tush

(Exeunt Pooh-Bah and Pish-Tush.)

Ko-Ko: This is simply appalling! I, who allowed myself to be respited at the last moment, simply in order to benefit my native town, am now required to die within a month, and that by a man whom I have loaded with honours! Is this public gratitude? Is this— *(Enter Nanki-Poo, with a rope in his hands.)* Go away, sir! How dare you? Am I never to be permitted to soliloquize?

N-Poo: Oh, go on — don't mind me.

Ko-Ko: What are you going to do with that rope?

N-Poo: I'm about to terminate an unendurable existence.

Ko-Ko: Terminate your existence? Oh, nonsense! What for?

N-Poo: Because you are going to marry the girl I adore.

Ko-Ko: Nonsense, sir. I won't permit it. I am a humane man; and if you attempt anything of the kind, I shall order your instant arrest. Come, sir, desist at once, or I summon my guard.

N-Poo: That's absurd. If you attempt to raise an alarm, I instantly perform the Happy Despatch with this dagger.

Ko-Ko: No, no, don't do that. This is horrible! *(Suddenly)* Why, you cold-blooded scoundrel, are you aware that, in taking your life, you are committing a crime which — which — which is — Oh! *(Struck by an idea)* Substitute!

N-Poo: What's the matter?

Ko-Ko: Is it *absolutely certain* that you are resolved to die?

N-Poo: Absolutely!

Ko-Ko: Will *nothing* shake your resolution?

N-Poo: Nothing.

Ko-Ko: Threats, entreaties, prayers — all useless?

N-Poo: All! My mind is made up.

Ko-Ko: Then, if you really mean what you say, and if you are absolutely resolved to die, and if nothing whatever will shake your determination — don't spoil yourself by committing suicide, but be beheaded handsomely at the hands of the Public Executioner!

N-Poo: I don't see how that would benefit me.

Ko-Ko: You don't? Observe: you'll have a month to live, and you'll live like a fighting cock at my expense. When the day comes, there'll be a grand public ceremonial — you'll be the central figure — no one will attempt to deprive you of that distinction. There'll be a procession — bands — dead-march — bells tolling — all the girls in tears — Yum-Yum distracted — then, when it's all over, general rejoicings, and a display of fireworks in the evening. *You* won't see them, but they'll be there all the same.

N-Poo: Do you think Yum-Yum would really be distracted at my death?

Ko-Ko: I am convinced of it. Bless you, she's the most tender-hearted little creature alive.

N-Poo: I should be sorry to cause her pain. Perhaps, after all, if I were to withdraw from Japan, and travel in Europe for a couple of years, I might contrive to forget her.

Ko-Ko: Oh, I don't think you could forget Yum-Yum so easily; and, after all, what is more miserable than a love-blighted life?

N-Poo: True.

Ko-Ko: Life without Yum-Yum — why, it seems absurd!

N-Poo: And yet there are a good many people in the world who have to endure it.

Ko-Ko: Poor devils, yes! You are quite right not to be of their number.

N-Poo: *(Suddenly)* I *won't* be of their number!

Ko-Ko: Noble fellow!

N-Poo: I'll tell you how we'll manage it. Let me marry Yum-Yum tomorrow, and in a month you may behead me.

Ko-Ko: No, no. I draw the line at Yum-Yum.

N-Poo: Very good. If you can draw the line, so can I. *(Preparing rope)*

Ko-Ko: Stop, stop — listen one moment — be reasonable. How can I consent to your marrying Yum-Yum if I'm going to marry her myself?

N-Poo: My good friend, she'll be a widow in a month, and you can marry her then.

Ko-Ko: That's true, of course. I quite see that. But, dear me! my position during the next month will be most unpleasant — most unpleasant.

N-Poo: Not half so unpleasant as my position at the end of it.

Ko-Ko: But — dear me! — well — I agree — after all, it's only putting off my wedding for a month. But you won't prejudice her against me, will you? You see, I've educated her to be my wife; she's been taught to regard me as a wise and good man. Now I shouldn't like her views on that point disturbed.

N-Poo: Trust me, she shall never learn the truth from me.

(Enter Chorus, Pooh-Bah, and Pish-Tush.)

Nº 11. "With Aspect Stern and Gloomy Stride"
Finale — Act One

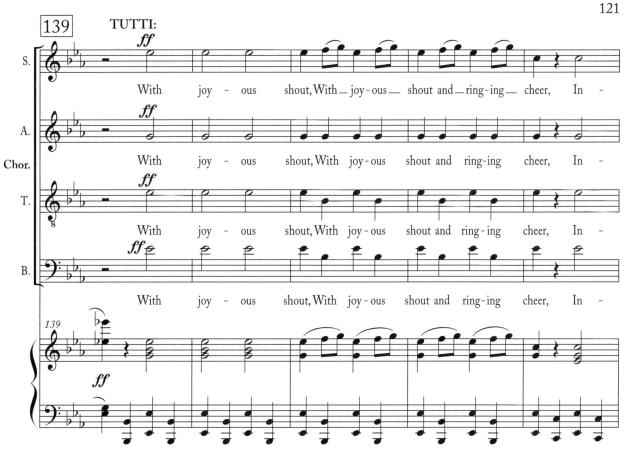

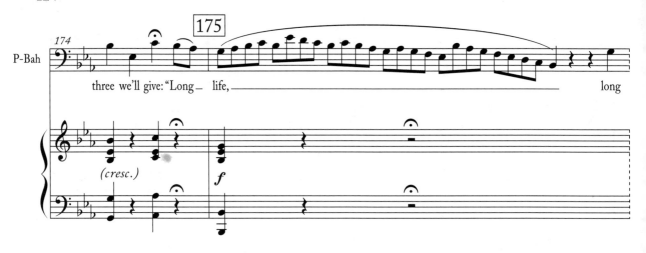

S. do, in all, all you do!

A. do! Long life to you— 'till then!

Chor. too, May you suc - ceed in all you do! Long life, long life to you—'till then!

T. too, May you suc - ceed in all you do! Long life, long life to you—'till then!

B. too, May you suc - ceed in all you do! Long life, long life to you—'till then!

193 (Dance)

(cresc.) — — — — — — *ff* *mf*

Allegro agitato ♩ = 80 (Enter Katisha, melodramatically.)

201

ff

(addressing Yum-Yum)

Kat. Pink cheek, that rul - est Where wis - dom base!

serves! Bright eye, that fool - est He - ro - ic nerves!

Rose lip, that scorn - est Lore - la - den years!

Smooth tongue, that warn - est Who right - ly hears! Thy

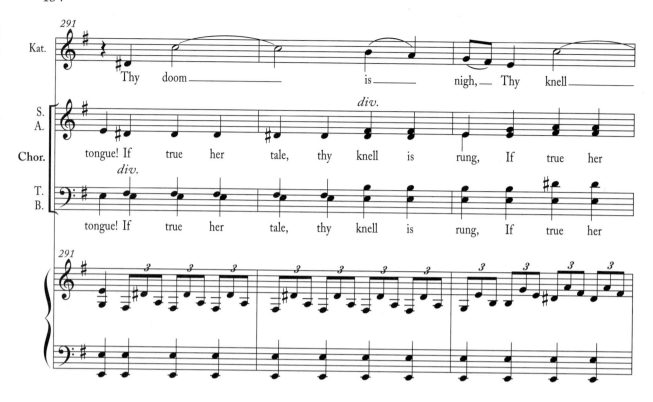

136

347

352 rall.

357 Andante Katisha:

Kat. The hour of glad - ness Is dead and gone; In si - lent

360

Kat. sad - ness I live a - lone! The hope I cher - ished All life - less

363 cresc.

Kat. lies, And all has per - ished, all has per - ished Save

cresc.

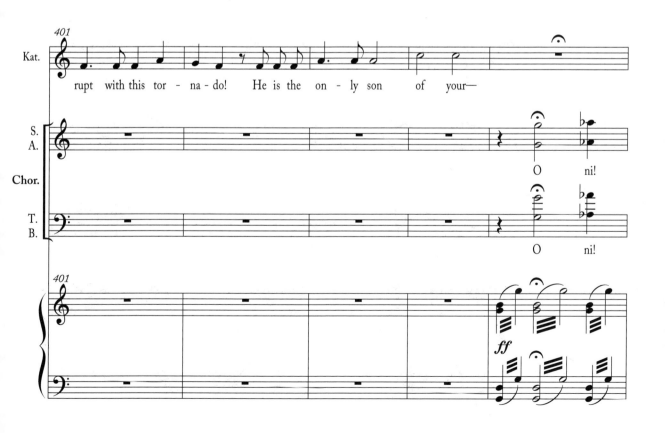

(Katisha rushes furiously up-stage, clearing the crowd away right and left, finishing on steps at back of stage.)

Curtain

End of Act One

Act Two

Scene: Ko-Ko's Garden. Yum-Yum discovered seated at her bridal toilet, surrounded by maidens, who are dressing her hair and painting her face and lips, as she judges of the effect in a mirror.

Nº 12. Chorus and Solo: "Braid the Raven Hair"
Pitti-Sing and Schoolgirls

S. Braid the ra - ven hair—Weave the sup - ple tress— Deck the mai - den fair— In her love - li - ness— Paint the pret - ty face— Dye the co - ral lip— Em - pha-size the

A. Braid the ra - ven hair—Weave the sup - ple tress— Deck the mai - den fair— In her love - li - ness— Paint the pret - ty face— Dye the co - ral lip— Em - pha-size the

(Exeunt Pitti-Sing, Peep-Bo and Chorus.)

Y-Yum: Yes, I am indeed beautiful! Sometimes I sit and wonder, in my artless Japanese way, why it is that I am so much more attractive than anybody else in the whole world. Can this be vanity? No! Nature is lovely and rejoices in her loveliness. I am a child of Nature, and take after my mother.

Nº 13. Song: "The Sun, Whose Rays Are All Ablaze"
Yum-Yum

162

(Enter Pitti-Sing and Peep-Bo.)

Y-Yum: Yes, everything seems to smile upon me. I am to be married today to the man I love best, and I believe I am the very happiest girl in Japan!

P-Bo: The happiest girl indeed, for she is indeed to be envied who has attained happiness in all but perfection.

Y-Yum: In "all but" perfection?

P-Bo: Well, dear, it can't be denied that the fact that your husband is to be beheaded in a month is, in its way, a drawback. It does seem to take the top off it, you know.

P-Sing: I don't know about that. It all depends!

P-Bo: At all events, he will find it a drawback.

P-Sing: Not necessarily. Bless you, it all depends!

Y-Yum: *(In tears)* I think it very indelicate of you to refer to such a subject on such a day. If my married happiness *is* to be — to be —

P-Bo: Cut short.

Y-Yum: Well, cut short — in a month, can't you let me forget it? *(Weeping)*

(Enter Nanki-Poo, followed by Pish-Tush.)

N-Poo: Yum-Yum in tears — and on her wedding-morn!

Y-Yum: *(Sobbing)* They've been reminding me that in a month you're to be beheaded! *(Bursts into tears)*

P-Sing: Yes, we've been reminding her that you're to be beheaded. *(Bursts into tears)*

P-Bo: It's quite true, you know, you are to be beheaded! *(Bursts into tears)*

N-Poo: *(Aside)* Humph! Now some bridegrooms would be depressed by this sort of thing! *(Aloud)* A month? Well, what's a month? Bah! These divisions of time are purely arbitrary. Who says twenty-four hours make a day?

P-Sing: There's a popular impression to that effect.

N-Poo: Then we'll efface it. We'll call each second a minute — each minute an hour — each hour a day — and each day a year. At that rate we've about thirty years of married happiness before us!

P-Bo: And, at that rate, this interview has already lasted four hours and three-quarters! *(Exit Peep-Bo.)*

Y-Yum: *(Still sobbing)* Yes. How time flies when one is thoroughly enjoying oneself!

N-Poo: That's the way to look at it! Don't let's be downhearted! There's a silver lining to every cloud.

Y-Yum: Certainly. Let's — let's be perfectly happy! *(Almost in tears)*

P-Tush: By all means. Let's — let's thoroughly enjoy ourselves.

P-Sing: It's — it's absurd to cry! *(Trying to force a laugh)*

Y-Yum: Quite ridiculous! *(Trying to laugh)*

(All break into a forced and melancholy laugh.)

Nº 14. Madrigal: "Brightly Dawns Our Wedding Day"
Yum-Yum, Pitti-Sing, Nanki-Poo, Pish-Tush

(Exeunt Pitti-Sing and Pish-Tush.)

(Nanki-Poo embraces Yum-Yum. Enter Ko-Ko. Nanki-Poo releases Yum-Yum.)

Ko-Ko: Go on— don't mind me.

N-Poo: I'm afraid we're distressing you.

Ko-Ko: Never mind, I must get used to it. Only please do it by degrees. Begin by putting your arm around her waist. *(Nanki-Poo does so.)* There! let me get used to that first.

Y-Yum: Oh, wouldn't you like to retire? It must pain you to see us so affectionate together!

Ko-Ko: No, I must learn to bear it! Now oblige me by allowing her head to rest on your shoulder.

N-Poo: Like that? *(He does so. Ko-Ko is much affected.)*

Ko-Ko: I am much obliged to you. Now— kiss her! *(He does so. Ko-Ko writhes with anguish.)* Thank you—it's simple torture!

Y-Yum: Come, come, bear up. After all, it's only for a month.

Ko-Ko: No. It's no use deluding oneself with false hopes.

N-Poo: What do you mean?

Y-Yum: What do you mean?

Ko-Ko: *(To Yum-Yum)* My child — my poor child! *(Aside)* How shall I break it to her? *(Aloud)* My little bride that was to have been—

Y-Yum: *(Delighted)* Was to have been?

Ko-Ko: Yes, you never can be mine!

N-Poo: *(in ecstasy)* What!

Y-Yum: I'm so glad!

Ko-Ko: I've just ascertained that, by the Mikado's law, when a married man is beheaded his wife is buried alive.

N-Poo: Buried alive!

Y-Yum: Buried alive!

Ko-Ko: Buried alive. It's a most unpleasant death.

N-Poo: But whom did you get that from?

Ko-Ko: Oh, from Pooh-Bah. He's my solicitor.

Y-Yum: But he may be mistaken!

Ko-Ko: So I thought; so I consulted the Attorney-General, the Lord Chief Justice, the Master of the Rolls, the Judge Ordinary, and the Lord Chancellor. They're all of the same opinion. Never knew such unanimity on a point of law in my life!

N-Poo: But stop a bit! This law has never been put in force.

Ko-Ko: Not yet. You see, flirting is the only crime punishable with decapitation, and married men never flirt.

N-Poo: Of course, they don't. I quite forgot that! Well, I suppose I may take it that my dream of happiness is at an end!

Y-Yum: Darling — I don't want to appear selfish, and I love you with all my heart — I don't suppose I shall ever love anybody else half as much — but when I agreed to marry you — my own — I had no idea — pet — that I should have to be buried alive in a month!

N-Poo: Nor I! It's the very first I've heard of it!

Y-Yum: It — it makes a difference, doesn't it?

N-Poo: It *does* make a difference, of course.

Y-Yum: You see — burial alive — it's such a stuffy death.

N-Poo: I call it a beast of a death.

Y-Yum: You see my difficulty, don't you?

N-Poo: Yes, and I see my own. If I insist on your carrying out your promise, I doom you to a hideous death; if I release you, you marry Ko-Ko at once.

Nº 14. Trio: "Here's a How-de-do"
Yum-Yum, Nanki-Poo, Ko-Ko

(Exit Yum-Yum.)

Ko-Ko: *(Going up to Nanki-Poo)* My poor boy, I'm really very sorry for you.

N-Poo: Thanks, old fellow. I'm sure you are.

Ko-Ko: You see I'm quite helpless.

N-Poo: I quite see that.

Ko-Ko: I can't conceive anything more distressing than to have one's marriage broken off at the last moment. But you shan't be disappointed of a wedding — you shall come to mine.

N-Poo: It's awfully kind of you, but that's impossible.

Ko-Ko: Why so?

N-Poo: Today I die.

Ko-Ko: What do you mean?

N-Poo: I can't live without Yum-Yum. This afternoon I perform the Happy Despatch.

Ko-Ko: No, no — pardon me — I can't allow that.

N-Poo: Why not?

Ko-Ko: Why, hang it all, you're under contract to die by the hand of the Public Executioner in a month's time! If you kill yourself, what's to become of me? Why, I shall have to be executed in your place!

N-Poo: It would certainly seem so!

(Enter Pooh-Bah.)

Ko-Ko: Now then, Lord Mayor, what is it?

P-Bah: The Mikado and his suite are approaching the city, and will be here in ten minutes.

Ko-Ko: The Mikado! He's coming to see whether his orders have been carried out!
(To Nanki-Poo) Now look here, you know — this is getting serious — a bargain's a bargain, and you really mustn't frustrate the ends of justice by committing suicide. As a man of honour and a gentleman, you are bound to die ignominiously by the hands of the Public Executioner.

N-Poo: Very well, then — behead me.

Ko-Ko: What, now?

N-Poo: Certainly; at once.

P-Bah: Chop it off! Chop it off!

Ko-Ko: My good sir, I don't go about prepared to execute gentlemen at a moment's notice. Why, I never even killed a blue-bottle!

P-Bah: Still, as Lord High Executioner —

Ko-Ko: My good sir, as Lord High Executioner I've got to behead him in a month. I'm not ready yet. I don't know how it's done. I'm going to take lessons. I mean to begin with a guinea pig, and work my way through the animal kingdom till I come to a Second Trombone. Why, you don't suppose that, as a humane man, I'd have accepted the post of Lord High Executioner if I hadn't thought the duties purely nominal? I can't kill you — I can't kill anything! I can't kill anybody! *(Weeps)*

N-Poo: Come, my poor fellow, we all have unpleasant duties to discharge at times; after all, what is it? If I don't mind, why should you? Remember, sooner or later it must be done.

Ko-Ko: *(Springing up suddenly) Must it?* I'm not so sure about that!

N-Poo: What do you mean?

Ko-Ko: Why should I kill you when making an affidavit that you've been executed will do just as well? Here are plenty of witnesses — the Lord Chief Justice, Lord High Admiral, Commander-in-Chief, Secretary of State for the Home Department, First Lord of the Treasury, and Chief Commissioner of Police.

N-Poo: But where are they?

Ko-Ko: There they are. They'll all swear to it — won't you? *(To Pooh-Bah)*

P-Bah: Am I to understand that all of us high Officers of State are required to perjure ourselves to ensure your safety?

Ko-Ko: Why not? You'll be grossly insulted, as usual.

P-Bah: Will the insult be cash down, or at a date?

Ko-Ko: It will be a ready-money transaction.

P-Bah: *(Aside)* Well, it will be a useful discipline. *(Aloud)* Very good. Choose your fiction, and I'll endorse it! *(Aside)* Ha! ha! Family Pride, how do you like *that*, my buck?

N-Poo: But I tell you that life without Yum-Yum—

Ko-Ko: Oh, Yum-Yum, Yum-Yum! Bother Yum-Yum! Here, Commissionaire *(to Pooh-Bah)*, go and fetch Yum-Yum. *(Exit Pooh-Bah)* Take Yum-Yum and marry Yum-Yum, only go away and never come back again. *(Enter Pooh-Bah with Yum-Yum)* Here she is. Yum-Yum, are you particularly busy?

Y-Yum: Not particularly.

Ko-Ko: You've five minutes to spare?

Y-Yum: Yes.

Ko-Ko: Then go along with his Grace the Archbishop of Titipu; he'll marry you at once.

Y-Yum: But if I'm to be buried alive?

Ko-Ko: Now, don't ask any questions, but do as I tell you, and Nanki-Poo will explain all.

N-Poo: But one moment—

Ko-Ko: Not for worlds. Here comes the Mikado, no doubt to ascertain whether I've obeyed his decree; and if he finds you alive I shall have the greatest difficulty in persuading him that I've beheaded you. *(Exeunt Nanki-Poo and Yum-Yum, followed by Pooh-Bah.)*

Close thing that, for here he comes!

(Exit Ko-Ko. Enter procession, heralding Mikado, with Katisha.)

Nº 16. Entrance of Mikado: "Miya Sama"
Mikado, Katisha, Schoolgirls, Noblemen, Guards and Servants

Begin on cue—"Now, don't ask any questions—"

Allegro Moderato ♩ = 80

S. A. *Chor.*

Mi - ya   sa - ma,   mi - ya   sa - ma,   On n'm-ma   no   ma - yé   ni   Pi - ra   Pi - ra   su - ro   no   wa

T. B.

Mi - ya   sa - ma,   mi - ya   sa - ma,   On n'm-ma   no   ma - yé   ni   Pi - ra   Pi - ra   su - ro   no   wa

N° 17. Song and Chorus: "A More Humane Mikado"

Mikado, Schoolgirls, Noblemen, Guards and Servants

41

Mik. pro - sy dull so - ci - e - ty sin-ners, Who chat-ter and bleat and bore,____ Are

Mik. sent to hear ser-mons From mys-ti-cal Ger-mans Who preach from ten till four. The

Mik. a - ma-teur te-nor, whose vo-cal vil-lain-ies All de-sire___ to shirk, Shall,

Mik. dur-ing off-hours,__ Ex - hib-it his pow-ers To Ma-dame Tus-saud's__ wax-work. The

(Enter Pooh-Bah, Ko-Ko, and Pitti-Sing. All kneel. Pooh-Bah hands a paper to Ko-Ko.)

Ko-Ko: I am honoured in being permitted to welcome your Majesty. I guess the object of your Majesty's visit—your wishes have been attended to. The execution has taken place.

Mik.: Oh, you've had an execution, have you?

Ko-Ko? Yes. The Coroner has just handed me his certificate.

P-Bah: I am the Coroner. *(Ko-Ko hands certificate to Mikado.)*

Mik.: And this is the certificate of his death. *(Reads)* "At Titipu, in the presence of the Lord Chancellor, Lord Chief Justice, Attorney General, Secretary of State for the Home Department, Lord Mayor, and Groom of the Second Floor Front—"

P-Bah: They were all present, your Majesty. I counted them myself.

Mik.: Very good house. I wish I'd been in time for the performance.

Ko-Ko: A tough fellow he was, too — a man of gigantic strength. His struggles were terrific. It was really a remarkable scene.

Mik.: Describe it.

Nº 18. Trio and Chorus: "The Criminal Cried as He Dropped Him Down"

Ko-Ko, Pitti-Sing, Pooh-Bah, Schoolgirls, Noblemen, Guards and Servants

199

*The low "Bs" in this measure and measures 87–88 should imitate the sound of a bass drum.

**Cue-size notes are sometimes omitted in some performance traditions.

204

(Exeunt Chorus.)

Mik.: All this is very interesting, and I should like to have seen it. But we came about a totally different matter. A year ago my son, the heir to the throne of Japan, bolted from our Imperial Court.

Ko-Ko: Indeed! Had he any reason to be dissatisfied with his position?

Kat.: None whatever. On the contrary, I was going to marry him — yet he fled!

P-Bah: I am surprised that he should have fled from one so lovely!

Kat.: That's not true.

P-Bah: No!

Kat.: You hold that I am not beautiful because my face is plain. But you know nothing; you are still unenlightened. Learn, then, that it is not in the face alone that beauty is to be sought. My face is unattractive!

P-Bah: It is.

Kat.: But I have a left shoulder-blade that is a miracle of loveliness. People come miles to see it. My right elbow has a fascination that few can resist.

P-Bah: Allow me!

Kat.: It is on view Tuesdays and Fridays, on presentation of visiting card. As for my circulation, it is the largest in the world.

Ko-Ko: And yet he fled!

Mik.: And is now masquerading in this town, disguised as a Second Trombone.

Ko-Ko, P-Bah, P-Sing: A Second Trombone!

Mik.: Yes; would it be troubling you too much if I asked you to produce him? He goes by the name of—

Kat.: Nanki-Poo.

Mik.: Nanki-Poo.

Ko-Ko: It's quite easy — that is, it's rather difficult. In point of fact, he's gone abroad!

Mik.: Gone abroad? His address!

Ko-Ko: Knightsbridge!

Kat.: *(Who is reading certificate of death)* Ha!

Mik.: What's the matter?

Kat.: See here — his name — Nanki-Poo — beheaded this morning. Oh, where shall I find another! Where shall I find another!

(Ko-Ko, Pooh-Bah, and Pitti-Sing fall on their knees.)

Mik.: *(Looking at paper)* Dear, dear, dear! this is very tiresome. *(To Ko-Ko)* My poor fellow, in your anxiety to carry out my wishes you have beheaded the heir to the throne of Japan!

Ko-Ko: I beg to offer an unqualified apology.

P-Bah: I desire to associate myself with that expression of regret.

P-Sing: We really hadn't the least notion—

Mik.: Of course you hadn't. How could you? Come, come, my good fellow, don't distress yourself — it was no fault of yours. If a man of exalted rank chooses to disguise himself as a Second Trombone, he must take the consequences. It really distresses me to see you take on so. I've no doubt he thoroughly deserved all he got. *(They rise.)*

Ko-Ko: We are infinitely obliged to your Majesty—

P-Sing: Much obliged, your Majesty.

P-Bah: Very much obliged, Your Majesty.

Mik.: Obliged? not a bit. Don't mention it. How *could* you tell?

P-Bah: No, of course we couldn't tell who the gentleman really was.

P-Sing: It wasn't written on his forehead, you know.

Ko-Ko: It might have been on his pocket-handkerchief, but Japanese don't use pocket-handkerchiefs! Ha! ha! ha!

Mik.: Ha! ha! ha! *(To Katisha)* I forget the punishment for compassing the death of the Heir Apparent.

Ko-Ko, P-Bah, P-Sing: Punishment! *(They drop down on their knees again.)*

Mik.: Yes. Something lingering, with boiling oil in it, I fancy. Something of that sort. I think boiling oil occurs in it, but I'm not sure. I know it's something humorous, but lingering, with either boiling oil or melted lead. Come, come, don't fret — I'm not a bit angry.

Ko-Ko: *(In abject terror)* If your Majesty will accept our assurance, we had no idea —

Mik.: Of course —

P-Sing: I knew nothing about it.

P-Bah: I wasn't there.

Mik.: That's the pathetic part of it. Unfortunately, the fool of an Act says "compassing the death of the Heir Apparent." There's not a word about a mistake —

Ko-Ko, P-Bah, P-Sing: No!

Mik.: Or not knowing —

Ko-Ko: No!

Mik.: Or having no notion —

P-Sing: No!

Mik.: Or not being there —

P-Bah: No!

Mik.: There should be, of course —

Ko-Ko, P-Bah, P-Sing: Yes!

Mik.: But there isn't.

Ko-Ko, P-Bah, P-Sing: Oh!

Mik.: That's the slovenly way in which these Acts are always drawn. However, cheer up, it'll be all right. I'll have it altered next session. Now, let's see about your execution — will after luncheon suit you? Can you wait till then?

Ko-Ko, P-Bah, P-Sing: Oh, yes — we can wait till then!

Mik.: Then we'll make it after luncheon.

P-Bah: I don't want any lunch.

Mik.: I'm really very sorry for you all, but it's an unjust world, and virtue is triumphant only in theatrical performances.

Nº 19. Glee: "See How the Fates Their Gifts Allot"
Mikado, Pitti-Sing, Pooh-Bah, Ko-Ko and Katisha

208

(Exeunt Mikado and Katisha.)

Ko-Ko: Well, a nice mess you've got us into, with your nodding head and the deference due to a man of pedigree!

P-Bah: Merely corroborative detail, intended to give artistic verisimilitude to an otherwise bald and unconvincing narrative.

P-Sing: Corroborative detail indeed! Corroborative fiddlestick!

Ko-Ko: And you're just as bad as he is with your cock-and-a-bull stories about catching his eye and his whistling an air. But that's so like you! You must put in your oar!

P-Bah: But how about your big right arm?

P-Sing: Yes, and your snickersnee!

Ko-Ko: Well, well, never mind that now. There's only one thing to be done. Nanki-Poo hasn't started yet— he must come to life again at once. *(Enter Nanki-Poo and Yum-Yum, prepared for journey.)* Here he comes. Here, Nanki-Poo, I've good news for you — you're reprieved.

N-Poo: Oh, but it's too late. I'm a dead man, and I'm off for my honeymoon.

Ko-Ko: Nonsense! A terrible thing has just happened. It seems you're the son of the Mikado.

N-Poo: Yes, but that happened some time ago.

Ko-Ko: Is this a time for airy persiflage? Your father is here, and with Katisha!

N-Poo: My father! and with Katisha!

Ko-Ko: Yes, he wants you particularly.

P-Bah: So does she.

Y-Yum: Oh, but he's married now.

Ko-Ko: But, bless my heart! what has that to do with it?

N-Poo: Katisha claims me in marriage, but I can't marry her because I'm married already — consequently she will insist on my execution; and if I'm executed, my wife will have to be buried alive.

Y-Yum: You see our difficulty.

Ko-Ko: Yes. I don't know what's to be done.

N-Poo: There's one chance for you. If you could persuade Katisha to marry you, she would have no further claim on me, and in that case I could come to life without any fear of being put to death.

Ko-Ko: I marry Katisha!

Y-Yum: I really think it's the only course.

Ko-Ko: But, my good girl, have you seen her? She's something appalling!

P-Sing: Ah! that's only her face. She has a left elbow which people come miles to see!

P-Bah: I am told that her right heel is much admired by connoisseurs.

Ko-Ko: My good sir, I decline to pin my heart upon any lady's right heel.

N-Poo: It comes to this: while Katisha is single, I prefer to be a disembodied spirit. When Katisha is married, existence will be as welcome as the flowers in spring.

Nº 20. Duet: "The Flowers That Bloom in the Spring"
Nanki-Poo, Ko-Ko with Yum-Yum, Pitti-Sing and Pooh-Bah

Ko-Ko: thing, Tra la, With a car-i-ca-ture of a face, With a car-i-ca-ture of a

Ko-Ko: face. And that's what I mean when I say, or I sing, "Oh, both-er the flow-ers that

Ko-Ko: bloom in the spring," Tra la la la la,—Tra la la la la,—"Oh, both-er the flow-ers of

219

Nº 21. Recitative and Song: "Alone, and Yet Alive!"
Katisha

* This G♯ is a B in the autograpg
** This G♯ is notated as F♯ in some editions.

Kat. hope is gone, Dost thou stay on?_____ Why lin-ger here, Where

Kat. all is drear? Oh, liv - ing I! Come, tell__ me_

Kat. why, When hope__ is gone, Dost thou stay on? May not a cheat-ed mai-den

Kat. die? May not__ a cheat-ed mai-den die?

Ko-Ko: *(Entering and approaching her timidly)* Katisha!

Kat.:   The miscreant who robbed me of my love! But vengeance pursues — they are heating the cauldron!

Ko-Ko.:   Katisha — behold a suppliant at your feet! Katisha — mercy!

Kat.:   Mercy? Had you mercy on him? See here, you! You have slain my love. He did not love *me,* but he would have loved me in time. I am an acquired taste — only the educated palate can appreciate *me.* I was educating *his* palate when he left me. Well, he is dead, and where shall I find another? It takes years to train a man to love me. Am I to go through the weary round again, and, at the same time, implore mercy for you who robbed me of my prey — I mean my pupil — just as his education was on the point of completion? Oh, where shall I find another?

Ko-Ko: *(Suddenly, and with great vehemence)* Here! — Here!

Kat.:   What!!!

Ko-Ko: *(With intense passion)* Katisha, for years I have loved you with a white-hot passion that is slowly but surely consuming my very vitals! Ah, shrink not from me! If there is aught of woman's mercy in your heart, turn not away from a love-sick suppliant whose every fibre thrills at your tiniest touch! True it is that, under a poor mask of disgust, I have endeavoured to conceal a passion whose inner fires are broiling the soul within me. But the fire will not be smothered — it defies all attempts at extinction, and, breaking forth, all the more eagerly for its long restraint, it declares itself in words that will not be weighed — that cannot be schooled — that should not be too severely criticized. Katisha, I dare not hope for your love — but I will not live without it! Darling!

Kat.:   You, whose hands still reek with the blood of my betrothed, dare to address words of passion to the woman you have so foully wronged!

Ko-Ko: I do — accept my love, or I perish on the spot!

Kat.:   Go to! Who knows so well as I that no one ever yet died of a broken heart!

Ko-Ko: You know not what you say. Listen!

224

Nº 22. Song: "Willow, Tit-Willow"
Ko-Ko

(During this song Katisha has been greatly affected, and at the end is almost in tears.)

Kat.: *(Whimpering)* Did he really die of love?

Ko-Ko: He really did.

Kat.: All on account of a cruel little hen?

Ko-Ko: Yes.

Kat.: Poor little chap!

Ko-Ko: It's an affecting tale, and quite true. I knew the bird intimately.

Kat.: Did you? He must have been very fond of her!

Ko-Ko: His devotion was something extraordinary.

Kat.: *(Still whimpering)* Poor little chap! And — and if I refuse you, will you go and do the same?

Ko-Ko: At once.

Kat.: No, no — you mustn't! Anything but that! *(Falls on his breast.)* Oh, I'm a silly little goose!

Ko-Ko: *(Making a wry face)* You are!

Kat.: And you won't hate me because I'm just a little teeny weeny wee bit bloodthirsty, will you?

Ko-Ko: Hate you? Oh, Katisha! is there not beauty even in bloodthirstiness?

Kat.: My idea exactly.

Nº 23. Duet: "There is Beauty in the Bellow of the Blast"

Katisha and Ko-Ko

(Flourish. Enter the Mikado, attended by Pish-Tush and Court.)

'Traditional' Fanfare

Fanfare

*New Fanfare orchestration
and arrangement by E. Jones*

Moderato ♩ = 116

Mik.:   Now then, we've had a capital lunch, and we're quite ready. Have all the painful preparations been made?

P-Tush: Your Majesty, all is prepared.

Mik.:   Then produce the unfortunate gentleman and his two well-meaning but misguided accomplices.

(Enter Katisha, Ko-Ko, Pitti-Sing, and Pooh-Bah. They throw themselves at the Mikado's feet.)

Kat.:   Mercy! Mercy for Ko-Ko! Mercy for Pitti-Sing! Mercy even for Pooh-Bah!

Mik.:   I beg your pardon, I don't think I quite caught that remark.

P-Bah: Mercy even for Pooh-Bah.

Kat.:   Mercy! My husband that was to have been is dead, and I have just married this miserable object.

Mik.:   Oh! You've not been long about it!

Ko-Ko: We were married before the Registrar.

P-Bah: *I* am the Registrar.

Mik.:   I see. But my difficulty is that, as you have slain the Heir Apparent—

(Enter Nanki-Poo and Yum-Yum. They kneel.)

N-Poo: The Heir Apparent is *not* slain.

Mik.:   Bless my heart, my son!

Y-Yum: And your daughter-in-law elected!

Kat.:   *(Seizing Ko-Ko)* Traitor, you have deceived me!

Mik.:   Yes, you are entitled to a little explanation, but I think he will give it better whole than in pieces.

Ko-Ko: Your Majesty, it's like this: it is true that I stated that I had killed Nanki-Poo—

Mik.:   Yes, with most affecting particulars.

P-Bah: Merely corroborative detail intended to give artistic verisimilitude to a bald and—

Ko-Ko: *Will* you refrain from putting in your oar? *(To Mikado)* It's like this: when your Majesty says, "Let a thing be done," it's as good as done — practically, it *is* done — because your Majesty's will is law. Your Majesty says, "Kill a gentleman," and a gentleman is told off to be killed. Consequently, that gentleman is as good as dead — practically, he *is* dead — and if he is dead, why not say so?

Mik.:   I see. Nothing could possibly be more satisfactory!

Nº 24. "For He's Gone and Married Yum-Yum"
Finale—Act Two

*The full score and the first edition have two high B♭s here.

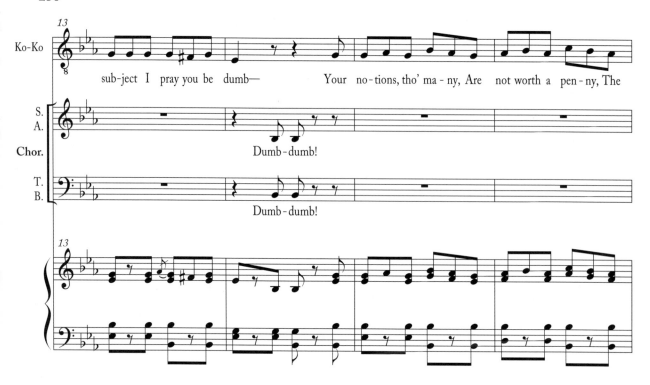

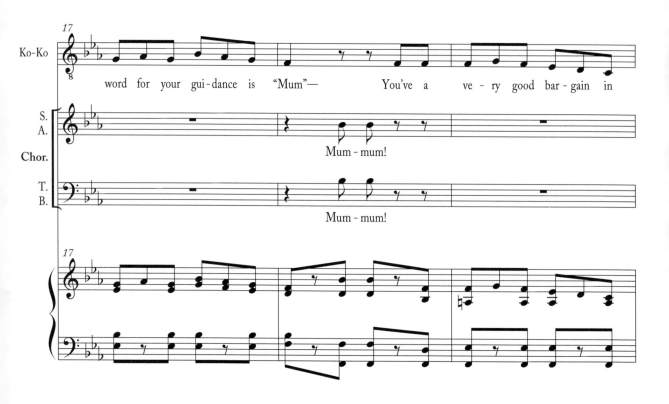

Curtain

End of Opera